A good book inspires you.

It can change your attitude and open you up to new experiences.

A good book can make us a better person and live a better life.

...Take time to say thanks how one object, held between two palms,
Can teach you what it means to be human and make you alive.

Mariska Van Aals

Dear Friend,

May this book serve to Motivate and Inspire you to fully LIVE your life to your highest potential.
I passionately care about getting you excited about your life, and assisting you in making choices that brings you closer to the person you long to be.
I have three questions for you:

Q. What's your purpose?
Find your passion. It is so important to love what you do and live magic moments.

Q. What's your action plan going to be?
Ignite the Energy to fuel the fire inside of you.

Q. What's your legacy?
The power of vision - your journey, your destination, your legacy.

Everyone has the power for greatness. Greatness is determined by knowing and finding your passion. You will feel it. Each of us has a unique call to greatness. Pay attention to what makes you feel energised and feel connected. You will become what you believe in, and unbelievable things will be attracted into your life.

Your mission - Should you choose to accept it...
Q. When would NOW... be a good time for you to choose who you want to become?

Satnav for the Soul

May this book serve to **Motivate** and **Inspire** you to fully **LIVE** your life to your highest potential.

Dedicated to my son Simon and my family…
so blessed we are part of each others lives.

Live in gratitude

by Susie Mitchell

Satnav for the Soul

My Voice Publishing
Unit 1 16 Maple Road
EASTBOURNE
BN23 6NY

www.myvoicepublishing.com

Published by MVP April 2007

© Sue Mitchell 2007

Sue Mitchell asserts the moral right to be identified as the author of this work

All rights reserved. No portion of this book may be used or reproduced in any manner whatsoever, except for brief quotations in critical reviews or articles, without prior written permission of the publisher.

Designed by Red Fred Limited
+ 44 (0) 1270 628525

Special thanks to Broomhay Secretarial Services
+ 44 (0) 1606 598000

ISBN 978-0-9554692-2-0

My Voice Publishing 2007

Satnav for the Soul

Q. What creates an extraordinary quality of life?
Q. What are the forces that shape the direction of our lives and ultimately our destiny?

There will be a moment when we make a choice in life… and it changes us forever.

a decision…

When people take action to make a positive change in their lives, a higher power intercedes on their behalf.

contents

Satnav for the Soul

- journey 8
- choices 12
- energy 20
- gratitude 28
- happiness 34
- passion 40
- relationships 46
- legacy 54
- incantations 60

journey

Q. What journey do you wish for your life?

Your life is a journey. No matter who we are or where we live, we all have our own journey. Your journey is a journey of learning. Live it fully and pay attention to life itself . Every choice gives us a chance to pave our own road. The gift is deciding who I could become - whether you flounder or flourish, the decision is always in your hands. You are the biggest single influence in your life, and your journey begins with a choice - to step up and fully embrace this dance of life!

Q. Where would I start if I was not afraid of making a mistake, feeling rejected, looking foolish or being alone?

Desires create the dreams that lead to your destiny.

The ' road map' of your journey needs to be thought through with how 'you want to live and be...'. No dream is too big - you just have to become the person the dream challenges you to be.

The journey begins by determining what it is you most desire and every journey requires preparation. You will need to focus on connecting with all aspects of YOU - your physical, mental, emotional and spiritual side, and learn how to overcome obstacles - such as unproductive beliefs and emotions. This will be discussed in the chapter about Energy, by accessing your magnetic and dynamic energies you will find the strength and the ability to attract all possibilities.

Journey   Satnav for the Soul

case study - mike...

Mike came to my coaching practice a couple of years ago, a young man of twenty five years young and wanted to find a direction for his life.

I took him through the 'rocking chair' test which enabled him to look back on his life and see that he had lived the best life he wanted for himself. Life is a journey and you certainly have to know what the final destination is and what you want to achieve.

> On one of our next sessions we went through the 'Wheel of Life', a tool that looks at all areas of life... such as health, career, finances, relationships.
>
> Mike chooses to concentrate on building his business for the first year and we set goals, targets and strategies to accomplish what he wanted. His business went from strength to strength and very soon he decided he wanted a lady in his life to share things with. I am very happy to say he met a wonderful lady Ruth, who has just moved in and I know he is whisking her off to the Maldives soon to propose!
>
> Life... can give you everything you desire... and at any time you can look at segments of your life, with focus and a clearly defined power of intention, you truly can set yourself on the destination to living a spectacular life!

> My promise to you...
> Start by honouring and respecting your heart that whatever excites you and makes you feel most alive will lead to your destiny.

Let your journey begin...

your journey

Do you reach beyond to touch the sky, or lag behind afraid to try?
Do you reach beyond to learn anew, or hesitate - the same old you?
Do you reach beyond to test your limit, or do you tell yourself, I'm timid?
Do you reach beyond to lead the pack, or do you waste time looking back?
Do you reach beyond and strive to find better ways to stretch your mind?
Do you reach beyond to care and share and help others do and dare?
Do you reach beyond, expect the best, or have you given up the quest?
Do you reach beyond and claim your space, here and now, this time, this place?
Do you reach beyond and try and soar, or, sadly, play it safe once more?

Suzy Sutton

choices

Q. What kind of life do you want and how close are you to living it?

Choices in life are a balancing act. We can all choose to do certain things every day of our lives. You can get a warm glow from changing your attitude to life.
Focus on what's important to your life and make positive changes to make you happy. We have to see life as an adventure. Each adventure is a chance to have fun, learn something, explore the world and broaden our horizons.

Be kind to yourself when you mess things up (we are only human after all!)

Q. Are you ready to make life your sparring partner?

Change your thinking and step outside of yourself. Every day we are faced with an immense number of choices and every action we make has an effect on our family, friends, society and the world in general - and that effect, can be positive or detrimental.

We get torn between what's good for us and what's good for others. No one said it would be easy. Life is a challenge - Thank God! It allows us to stretch and grow, it moulds us into a better person. If it was easy we would get bored. Only dead fish swim with the stream - 'live' fish swim against the currents! Each flick of the fin makes us stronger.

Q. Which fish do you want to become?

Change what you can change and let go of the rest. Time is short and do not waste any of it. Aim to be the very best of everything you can be. If you are a parent, be the best parent. If you go to work, be the best at what you do. Set your own standard and leave a little space for yourself each day. Know where true happiness comes from. Look after yourself. You are the Boss and Captain of your own ship.

Here are some areas that you can focus on for the choices in your life:

1. You can choose where to be.
2. You can choose how to act.
3. You can choose who you trust.
4. You can choose who you avoid.
5. You can choose what to say and what to do.
6. You can choose what to believe and you can choose what to say about yourself.
7. You can choose what to say about others.
8. You can choose what behaviour to have day to day.

Q. What choices are you going to make in all areas of your life?

Get real with yourself about your life and everybody in it. Be truthful about what isn't working in your life and start getting results.

If you are unwilling to acknowledge a thought, a circumstance, a problem, behaviour or emotion; if you do not take ownership in any situation, then you cannot and will not change it. You cannot change what you do not acknowledge. Denial kills hope.

You can choose and create your own experience. It takes courage and commitment to be genuinely honest with yourself.

You cannot and will not spend another day not doing what you want - what you truly want. You also give yourself permission to be less then perfect.

It is the meaning we give to the events - we can choose positively or choose to be negative. We can choose how we perceive them. Taking Action is part of the formulae of living a fulfilling life -

BE - DO - HAVE
BE committed to DO what it takes, and you will HAVE what you want

Q. What/Who are you willing to Be, Do and Have ?

Decide now that you will take the risk, make the effort, and be persistent in the pursuit of your dreams and goals. Your life will be filled with victories and rewards.

Take actions and insist on results.

You will have values that will be incorporated into the core of your soul. You will live them daily. Have a high standard of what you want out of life. Step out of your comfort zone. A great daily question could be:

Q. What can I do today to make my life better?

Ask it each and every day. Raise the bar. Your thinking needs to stay focused but flexible. Demand those special things, amazing feelings and outstanding magic experiences.

Be very clear about what you want, and very clear about what you don't want.

This is an important distinction : If you can recognise it not the thing or event that you really want, but the FEELINGS that you associate with it, then your goal shifts from the thing or the event, to the EMOTIONS that are connected with them.

I believe these magic ingredients make an outstanding person:
Outstanding psychology, Outstanding Physiology, Empower yourself and others, Passion, A hunter of human excellence, and Presence.

Don't ask yourself what the world needs - ask yourself what makes you come alive, and go do that, because the world needs people who are alive!

case study - mary...

Mary came to me struggling with finances. She was in a mess and could not afford to pay her mortgage and was steeped in debt.

I established that this had been a pattern over her entire life thus far... she had reached the end of her tether and realised she must change. Her husband was on the verge of divorce due to her frivolous spending and her children despaired with her.

Using various tools and techniques I found out the reasons why Mary had been spending and we set about a plan of action.

Today Mary is debt free, and adopting new patterns of spending within her limits, and her husband is totally in love with her again as she has become a new woman!

We all have many choices in our life. We have to decide, are they good for us and good for others. I believe we should always make the choices from two perceptions, us and others.

My promise to you...

Finding your formulae is the key to your success.

You are unique in how you choose to navigate your life. Your formula is like a recipe: have the vision - th purpose.

Find the strategy.

When you begin to use your energy, have faith in yc passion, and totally trust in your purpose, you will liv SPECTACULAR life !

Make the choices that are right for YOU!

your choices

Our choices in life? What is your calling?
What I know for sure – If you ask the question the answer will come.
You have to be willing to listen for the answer.
You have to get still enough to hear the choices, to pay attention.
Through the truth of who you are and what you can be...
Listen to your choice.

Oprah

energy

give energy - get energy!

Q. Are you doing everything with enthusiasm?

We can teach ourselves how to live spectacularly now, right in the heart of this moment. When we nourish each fresh experience, we have all our juices flowing. The inner spark is infectious !
The way to increase our energy is to find lots and lots of things to be enthusiastic about.
Enthusiasm is an internal emotional state. We get good vibes by giving them- Being around people who exude positive energy is stimulating and inspiring.
Good feelings are great energy boosters.

Q. On a scale of 1-10 where is your energy level?

Knowing and understanding our energy level is key to freeing great resources of positive feelings.
Be tuned into your natural energy surges - through visual, sounds and touch.
Know what fills you - and what drains you.
Give and take is the law of universal energy - the natural dance of life. The deepest happiness comes from caring and helping others, coming from our heart.
To understand our place in the world, we recognise that we are here to play our unique part, to use our gifts and talents to feel truly connected to other living souls. We are not a one man band - we are part of a huge well tuned orchestra of life.
The more loving energy we generate, the happier we become.

Q. How do we arrive at a place in our lives where we feel so 'alive' and 'juiced' - that every day is an outstanding day?

Science tell us that the universe vibrates with the same force of energy that created it in the first place. When we raise our level of consciousness, and work in partnership with this energy, we live a blessed and magic life!

One of my beliefs (and you could take it on as one of yours!) is that I believe my life is guided by a force that gives me amazing energy. This energy is available to us each and every moment we choose. When we connect with this, I believe we step into a larger arena to play in. We become aware of signs and messages that leads us to our highest good. It is becoming known as The Power of Intention - where anything becomes possible. Open your eyes and heart to a new way of looking at yourself and the world.

Q. What is your power of Intention ?

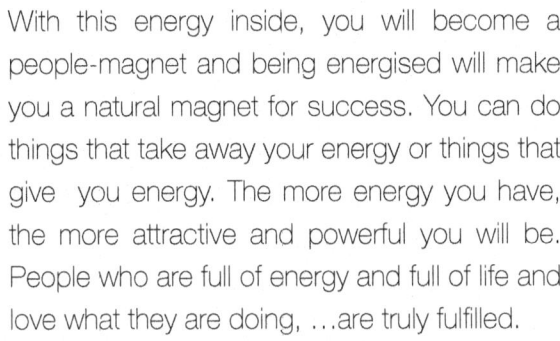

With this energy inside, you will become a people-magnet and being energised will make you a natural magnet for success. You can do things that take away your energy or things that give you energy. The more energy you have, the more attractive and powerful you will be. People who are full of energy and full of life and love what they are doing, ...are truly fulfilled.

Some of my clients say they are 'stuck' at a place in their lives... And they do not know how to move forward. It is not possible to stand still or be stuck if you kick energy into your life. Energy (and therefore life) is always in motion. Things are always changing. If you continue to think the same thoughts, do the same things and feel the same things - you will stay stuck...

so... if you want things to change...

Q. What different thoughts are you going to have, what things are you prepared to do, and how differently are you going to feel?

You will start attracting people into your life that support your needs and inspire your personal growth. This will help you to become healthy and a more connected, conscious human being.

Every day we receive ' intuitive nudges', feelings or messages- our inner voice. Learn to listen to it. The quality of our life is determined by the quality of our emotions. For as long as we take breath into our bodies and have life in our being, emotions will happen as part of being human. We have the choice to feel positive emotions, or a choice to feel negative emotions.

Our greatest resource as a human being is the power of emotion. The foundation of all happiness, joy, love, passion, and fulfilment comes from our ability to harness the power of emotion and to train ourselves to become emotionally fit.

Q. What empowering and resourceful emotions are you feeling?

Q. What are some things you could do to positively intensify these feelings?

Your thoughts direct energy towards manifestation. You can control and direct whether that energy is positive or negative. The way you express yourself matters not only to you, but also to the universe.

Positive thoughts are so powerful and encouraging that the more you think them, the more you will be inspired to do the work of shifting from negative to positive every time. Your thoughts are behaviours too. Choosing thoughts contributes to your experiences, because when you choose your thoughts, you choose consequences that are associated with those thoughts. There is a very powerful connection at work here. Your physiology determines your energy and action level.

Q. So, how powerfully are your thoughts programming You?

The law of attraction says that we attract into our lives the things we believe we deserve at a deep level. If you want something in life, visualise and affirm it coming into your life. By being strong and centred you will empower yourself to accept that abundance is natural and easily comes to you.

We create our own experience. So acknowledge and accept accountability for your life. Understand your role in creating the results that you have in your life and what you want. The person you spend most time with is you. So the person you most need the power to influence and control is you!

Energy | Satnav for the Soul

case study - simon...

Simon has been struggling with so many areas of his life. He gets bored and changes focus very easily. He has his own business in the property field.

I could clearly see he needed to have more energy in his life, from his health and fitness goals... to his passion for his business.

We set tasks to engage in some form of exercise three times a week. Simon was motivated to look at his diet and stop eating and drinking things that were not good for him. After a short few weeks his energy was magnetic... and he was bounding out of bed in the mornings, and surprise, surprise his business was taking off in all directions.

When you are full of positive energy, you light up like a light bulb and it attracts great people into your life. People want to be around you as it makes them feel good!

The people who are in your circle of influence can either be positive or a negative drain... I truly suggest you decide to fly with the 'eagles' of life, and not hangaround with the 'turkeys'!

> ## My promise to you...
> You are a student in the school of life. Take advanta[ge] of the opportunities that arise.
> You have what it takes to face any life's challenges. Sometimes our greatest challenges will be our grea[test] blessing.
> You have the peace and happiness you desire insid[e] you.
> Use the energy you have inside you to fuel whatev[er] you want !

energy

Energy is the power that drives every human being.
Having the amazing physical and mental energy -
Will allow you to live a spectacular life!

Susie Mitchell

gratitude

Q. Are you living in gratitude of your gift of life?

Gratitude is the most passionate transformative force in the cosmos.
Gratitude unlocks the fullness of life. It turns what we have into enough, and more. It turns denial into acceptance, chaos to order, confusion to clarity: - it can turn a meal into a feast, a house into a home, a stranger into a friend.
Gratitude makes sense of our past, brings peace for today, and creates a vision for tomorrow.
Gratitude is an authentic awakening: you already possess all you need to be genuinely happy. All you truly need is the awareness of all you have.
Feeling grateful or appreciative of someone or something in your life actually attracts more of the things that you appreciate and value in your life. And the more of your life that you like and appreciate, the healthier you'll be. Science is now documenting that 'thinking with your heart' will lead you in the right direction.

Q. Who do you really appreciate in your life right now?

One of the main reasons most people do not have what they want in their life, is because they are not grateful for what they already have. When we focus on being blessed and grateful for the things we have in our life - it makes us 'think' in the 'NOW'... and we pay attention to the best of our life - this makes us feel good, and great feelings lead to great emotions. Gratitude drives emotions of belief and faith... and being thankful for what we have... is Gratitude.

> Create Magic moments... keep a 'magic moment journal' to record spectacular events and times of your life.

Q. Can you remember some outstanding magic moments in your life?

Gratitude is available the instant you bring all your awareness to this moment and really open up who you are to experience what is here. In order for gratitude to be true and real, there must be total acceptance of where you are right now - even though it may not be exactly where you want to be - by embracing it fully inside you, this allows you to accept life's blessings and if you really experience this, your heart will open up to more than you could ever want and dream about.

Q. Why not take time now to truly think about everything you are most grateful for in your life and voice it out loud?

case study - david...

David had been carrying a burden of his son's suicide for so long. His son died three years ago and he has been carrying the guilt inside him for all this time.

Through a powerful technique, David freed himself of the guilt and has gone onto to grieve in the normal way. He now sees his son in his grandchildren who daily fill his life with joy and fun!

He thanks God every day now for the time he had with his son... and with reflection I got David to see the many of life's lessons his son had taught him. He passes these to his grand children who keep the memory of their father alive.

We should be 'living in gratitude' everyday, to be grateful for the beautiful flowers and the things that are on this beautiful earth. We should be grateful for all the people we meet in our lifetime, and cherish our time spent with them.

Our focus should be on what's wonderful in our life, not the negative feelings and struggles.

Strive to be grateful daily, and you will be amazed how enriched your life will be.

> My promise to you...
> Gratitude is a choice.
> Gratitude can make the impossible happen, it has the power to bring about whatever your heart truly desires. (Choose wisely!)
> By choosing gratitude daily in your life, your life will be so rich with happiness, joy and whatever other empowering emotion you choose to feel. This true alignment of 'you' will resonate with the cosmos and you will be blessed with living a spectacular enriched life!

gratitude

I believe we were put on this earth to live a life of joy and abundance.
Be grateful for every day you live… And in our latter years…
Thank God for letting you be you!

Susie Mitchell

happiness

Q. Are you celebrating your life with laughter and fun?

The three essentials to happiness in life are something to do, something to love, and something to hope for.
Happiness lies in the passions we pursue and the pressures we decline. Happiness is what you make it, and where you make it.
Choosing happiness for ourselves and wishing to spread joy to others is the healthiest, wisest and most noble way to live our lives. Develop the capacity to be fully present in each moment and we will live a life of greater depth and meaning. Awaken all your senses to each fresh experience.

Write down 10 defining words that defines who you are - i.e. love, passion

> Magical things happen everyday if we allow it. We should aspire to live up to our higher, happier power. When we are happy we are in touch with our greatest human potential. We have to go for it do whatever makes our juices flow.

Q. What in your life makes you happy?
Say out loud everything or write it down

To be happy and obtain lasting happiness, we need to find out the truth of who we are.

Inner intelligence deepens our experiences and gives our life greater meaning.

The way to become more self-aware is to tap into our intuition - our inner guidance, for clarity and vision. Our intuition leads the way for our other five senses to teach us more about ourselves.

The secret of happiness is that it is always a choice. When we are happy we are living the life we are meant to be living.

There is a huge difference between expecting happiness to come to you because you deserve it, and going out and getting the happiness you believe you deserve.

Happiness is always now, and always a journey.

case study - john...

John was working for a manufacturing company and not fulfilled in his job, treading water on a daily basis.

After a few business development sessions, John made a decision to work for himself.

His eyes lit up each time he talked about starting his own business, realising he could spend more time with his family than the crazy long hours at the office.

Understand, John knew he had to work hard setting up his company, but he also knew he had the support of his wife and could proportion his time accordingly.

Decisions had to be made and a strategy to come out of the workplace was put into place.

John has been running his business for a year now and is living the life he had dreamt about for so long .John realised anything is possibly and after setting out 'what would make him truly happy',

We are here for a period of time, and surely we need to be living daily by our values and caring about others who are in our lives.

> ## My promise to you...
> Our lives are made up of a thousand thoughts, choices and steps we take every day. We can link them together to make them a brilliant reflection of our dreams... Our highest aspirations. When we choose happiness, we choose love. Open the door to happiness and enjoy an amazing spectacular life !

happiness

Happiness lies in the passions we pursue, and in the pressure we decline.
It is in the knowing how to work and when to play.
It is in the treasured objects we keep nearby,
And in the ordinary moments we elevate into celebrations.
It is a note we write to a friend, and the kindness we show a stranger.
Happiness is what you make it, where you make it.
Happiness is our best choice.

Alexandra Stoddard

passion

Q. Are you finding and pursuing your passion?

My definition of passion is to live your life fully and completely. It is to make up each morning and feel 'alive'!

The world will always present you with challenges. You can choose to live fully, giving your unique gifts to the world , or… You can choose to live out of balance.

We all have fears, we need to make fear our 'friend' so we can push through it and find the beauty on the other side. Fear of fear may lead you to live a lesser life than you are capable of… By leaning just beyond your fear, you challenge your limits - you step beyond the solid ground of security with an open heart.

Own your fear and lean just beyond it - In every aspect of your life!

Q. When do you want to start feeling truly fulfilled?

Honour the choices you make.
Make your life an ongoing process of being who you are, at your deepest level.
The core of your life is to find your purpose. Sometimes we start out not knowing what this is… And we may start a job/business wondering if this is truly what we are meant to do. The question is that I believe you will find out as time goes on if it is, and no one said you could not adjust the sails…

Q. Who is the Captain of your ship?

Everything in your life, from your diet to your career must be aligned with who you are. If you know your passion, your deepest desires, then the secret to success is to discipline your life so you support your deepest purpose and minimise distractions and detours.

If you do not know your deepest desires, then you cannot align your life to it. Everything in your life will be disassociated from your core. Disconnected from your core will make you feel weak and you will feel incomplete.

When you KNOW your true passion and purpose - every moment will be lived to express your core desires and you will be living your truth.

When would now be a good time to start finding and living your true passion/purpose?

case study - peter...

Peter had decided to start a business in computers. He built a team around him and over a few years it was building steadily. He used to question on a regular basis if this was definitely the business he should be in, as some days he did not want to go to work.

He was referred to me through a friend, and we worked through what Peter really wanted and the reason why he was building this computer business.

He just knew that he had a very creative mind and wanted to bring the leading edge of technology to the industry.

Sometimes things start out as a job, or as something we struggle with, but over time this changes into consuming passion, knowing we are on the right tract.

His passion is huge and he is a great motivator with his staff.

After working with Peter on his goals and aspirations, and holding him accountable to his achievements, I now work with his team, to motivate, inspire, cajole and strategise, and soar the people to new heights!

When someone knows their passion and purpose in life, they can become unstoppable!

My promise to you...

Start being passionate about everything you do and you will feel so good each and every day.

Put passion as one of your top values and see what a difference it makes.

passion

Passion powers our souls -
Without our hearts go hungry.
To find your passion,
Open your heart and let the world flood in.

Julia Vantine

relationships

Relationships

Q. Who are the people you choose to like, love and play with in your life?

Be your own shining star! Fill it bright inside you. Before you can have a relationship with another human being, you need to have the best relationship with yourself. Know who you are, fill yourself with feelings, emotions, compassion to yourself and feel yourself shifting deeper to loving yourself, and before you know it you will understanding, empathy, caring and love to another person.

Whether its relationships with people we love, friends, people we work with - each and every person deserves our respect, caring and love.

Connection is a powerful source. I know for sure that the way to feel connected in all relationships, is to stay attuned into your own self, or what we call source. This is our own unique energy that vibrates in all our lives. You can never stray far away from what is really meaningful, otherwise you loose connection with yourself and everyone else.

Listen to the thoughts inside you. When you connect with another person - really listen to them. Treasure each moment as other people have important lessons of life to teach us.

Q. Who matters in your life right now? Think about who you care about.

With relationships we learn how to control how we connect to people at a deeper level. We need to live to our highest values and align our beliefs to have our experiences along the way that will pull us in the direction of our ultimate vision of our lives.

One of our goals is to have strengths in as many areas of our lives as possible, as no two people are the same, and learning to connect and learn from others will weave a wonderful tapestry of life. Some of us may be naturally strong in our ability to connect with others, while another person's strengths may be paying attention to detail, and yet another's may be innovation and creation. We need a mixture of talents, knowledge and skills.

Q. What key strengths do you have in your human relationships?

> Everything we do is connected with people in some shape of form. Once you learn how people tick - you will understand the ' push and pull' of people. You will know how to turn situations around. You will understand how to change behaviour.
>
> Before you can truly connect with someone, you need to know how they tick inside…

Q. What key strengths do you have in your human relationships?

You either get it, or you don't get it. To become one of the people who get it, find out what makes people tick. Learn why you and other people do what they do, and don't do what they don't. Your job is to find out what 'it' is. You must be willing to learn some things you don't know, so that you can begin to make better choices and decisions.

The primary goal is to have the quality of experiences that are unique and rewarding. The skills that you need to create the quality of life, are the skills of understanding and controlling the 'cause and effect' of relationships of life. Using your knowledge to make things happen the way you want them to.

Think about people who are successful in the world. Most of them know how to get others to do things they want or need them to do. They know what buttons to push to get people to go in a certain direction, adopt their ideas, values and beliefs. They have mastered the understanding of human behaviour.

Here are some great questions I suggest you use to get to know others…
A good start would be to ask YOU them first!

Q. What is most important to you in life?

Q. What sort of things do you like to do in life?

Q. What are your expectations and beliefs about what life is and how it should work?

Q. How do you feel about yourself?

Q. What do you want most in life?

case study - sarah...

Sarah came to me lacking in self confidence and assertiveness. Her husband was about to take a serious role in the local government and she was expected to be alongside him at dinners and meeting people in the local community.

First of all Sarah needed to change the relationship she had with the most important person – herself!

Going back to her childhood, I discovered she had lost her confidence by her parents telling her consistently that she was not good enough. At school she never quite made the grade, (sadly being measured by her parent's standards) and her parents said she would never aspire to great things.

Using techniques to change associations and her past conditioning Sarah blossomed into a very confident, strong and self-assertive woman! She is now a recognised figure in her local community and Sarah's husband is proud to have her alongside him at the functions. She very quickly formed wonderful relationships with people and now people seek her out for advice and support.

Connection is a very powerful force, we all want to be loved, cared for and respected, so therefore it is imperative we learn the art of building successful relationships.

My promise to you...

Commit to be a student of human nature. Learn how people operate. Study people - it's all about attitude. Gather information daily and weave it into helping you to form better and more fulfilling relationships with people. This will enable you to be true to yourself and attract outstanding relationships into your life.

relationships

A hug is more than a physical touch.
It is a lightening... like a connection between two people.
A link that expresses love, encouragement, comfort...
All the emotions that can turn a life around...
A hug – an incredible gift that should be shared.

Kevin Ireland

legacy

Q. Are you growing daily in a deeper commitment to your life?

> With my clients we do the 'Rocking Chair' Test.
>
> Imagine at age 90 years young, and you are sitting in your rocking chair and reflecting back on your life... thinking of all the things that have happened to you and all the people who you have connected with and have met, the friends you have made along the journey of life... Would you do anything different... Would NOW be a good time...

Take time now to do the Rocking Chair test.

We want to make a better world for ourselves, family and friends.

Therefore we have to take responsibility for how we are going to live our life.

To know what counts and what does not. You have to know what you are dedicating your life to - it makes the rest easier.

As we go through life, we want to navigate ourselves towards new horizons; we want to embrace our transformation of who we are becoming, embody our destiny and to leave a long-term legacy.

We want to revolutionise our relationships and when everything we say, think, feel, want and do is directed towards a very powerful end. Imagine feeling that you are the master of your own experience - totally controlling every moment of your life.

Q. How do you feel in your heart of hearts what history is going to say about you after you are gone? Say out loud or write down.

We live in a time of discovery, where we are finding the human mind has far more capacity and ability than we ever imagined.

The concept of defining your legacy is something I am passionate about. I want you to know you have a choice. Each of us possess the will to create our own legacy. Its all a choice. Create the power to live the life of your choosing.

Loving people is part of the plan of life. When you make loving others the story of your life, there never is a final chapter- because the legacy goes on and on and on.

leaving a legacy

I am making this last chapter a personal one.

My grandmother is still alive at one hundred and three years young! She is totally together in her mind even though her body is beginning to shut down. When she was eighty, I asked her to narrate her life's story as it certainly is a fascinating one.

She was born and grew up in Wales, walking six miles to school each day with no heating or electricity in those days! (We would shudder what our grandparents went through) At the age of eighteen she became a maid in a stately home in the Midlands. There she met my grandfather who was an officer in the Welsh Guards. He was stationed oversees in China, and for five long years they corresponded by letter and then he returned and made her his bride.

They flew out to China and lived well until they were interned by the war. They were 'prisoners of war', and lived for four years in a camp run by the Japanese. My mother and uncle also lived through some horrendous atrocities.

After the war, they lived in Malaya and eventually came back to Wales. My grandfather died at the young age of sixty and my grandmother has been on her own for forty three years.

The reason I am sharing this story with you is that my grandmother has always taught me to live my life to the full. She has always said to be who you are, touch people's lives and leave 'you' on the imprint of time.

I know I am living my life the way I want to , helping others which I believe is my purpose, and knowing when I sit in my rocking chair at 103 (on earth or in heaven!) I can look back and know I have left a legacy.

Decide how you want to live YOUR life, so you can be remembered by your children and grandchildren, and may God bless you in whatever you choose!

> My promise to you...
> Seasons come and go. Every moment that you live it - enjoy it. Relish each day as if there would never be another, and when you get the chance to 'sit it out or dance' with life... I hope you dance!!

legacy

I love and approve of myself!
As long as you keep in mind the importance and value of you...
You will handle anything that the world throws your way.
You will succeed because of the power, the spirit, and the vision of 'you'.

Kara Messinger

incantations

Incantations have made a big difference in my life… and I challenge you to do them for one month… and see what happens…

An Incantation is a phrase or language pattern that is said out loud, using energy and engaging your body.

Incantations are one of the most powerful tools available for conditioning new beliefs, identity and language patterns.

Speak them aloud with volume and intensity. This embodies the emotions and beliefs that this incantation is declaring with absolute conviction and a sense of ownership. You must not only feel the true meaning of your incantation, but you must experience its rewards as you recite it. Use your gestures, your breathing, your facial expressions and body movement.

Repetition causes the incantation to become a thought inside that becomes a habit.

It needs to be said over and over again, as many times a day as possible to become engraved in your neurology.

It is proven that if something is consistely done for 21 days, it becomes a habit.

The more you consistently use all five senses as you declare, experience, feel and own this new belief (incantation), the more rapidly you will integrate it as your constant emotion, belief and identity.

some examples…

I am open to receive the power of grace in my life now. I ask to be shown examples of this in my life.

I am in the process of attracting my ideal partner into my life.

I am attracting Wealth and Financial Abundance into my life.

I celebrate my life daily with laughter and fun!

I am a good, kind and caring person.

Money flows easily and effortlessly into my life.

I make wise and fantastic choices daily that are aligned with my purpose.

I create many opportunities in my life.

I believe in myself.

I can find a way to live my dreams.

There is an divine energy working in me NOW!

incantations

Music can heal the soul...
All you have to do is ... Listen.

David Joachim

in conclusion

Listen to your heart and soul.

Do not deny the world of your gifts.

May you always have:
Enough happiness to keep you sweet;
Enough trials to keep you strong;
Enough success to keep you eager;
Enough faith to give you courage;
& enough determination to make each day a good day.

dance! as though no one is watching you

love! as though you have never been hurt

sing! as though no one can hear you

live! as though heaven is on earth!

My invitation to you…

…is to send me an email to share your emotions, your stories and your journey.
Send it to: info@susiemitchell.co.uk or visit my website: www.susiemitchell.co.uk

Journal Notes   Satnav for the Soul

Leave a legacy - use these pages to make a note of your own journey. Read it back when you have reached your destination and see how far you have come…

Journal Notes

Satnav for the Soul

Journal Notes

Journal Notes   Satnav for the Soul

Journal Notes · Satnav for the Soul

Lightning Source UK Ltd.
Milton Keynes UK
UKOW04f0614121017
310829UK00001BA/33/P